Project INDEPENDENCE:
After 56 Years

Clyde Weatherhead

**Project INDEPENDENCE:
After 56 Years**

OTHER PUBLICATIONS BY THE AUTHOR

Speaking Out: A Collection of Letters and Other Writings - 1991 – 1993, 2018 (paperback and kindle editions)

The Future of Mas: Children of the Carnival (Images from the Children's Carnival 2006 (kindle edition)

The Trinidad Carnival: Not Just Carnival in Trinidad, 2019 (paperback and kindle editions)

Available on Amazon

*To the Patriots who fought for the
Independence of Trinidad and Tobago,
to the youth of 1970 and all the
builders of Project Independence*

Contents

List of Abbreviations

ATSEFTWU	All Trinidad Sugar Estates and Factories Workers Union
COLA	Cost of Living Allowance
CSA	Civil Service Association
DAC	Democratic Action Congress
DEWD	Development Employment Works Programme
DLP	Democratic Labour Party
ISCOTT	Iron and Steel Company of Trinidad and Tobago
NAPA	National Academy of the Performing Arts
NAR	National Alliance for Reconstruction
NATUC	National Trade Union Centre
NJAC	National Joint Action Committee
OWTU	Oilfields Workers Trade Union
PDP	People's Democratic Party
PNM	People's National Movement
POPPG	Political Progress Group
PP	People's Partnership
PTSC	Public Transport Service Corporation
SOPO	Summit of People's Organisations
TECA	Teachers' Economic and Cultural Association
TelCo	Trinidad and Tobago Telephone Company Limited
TIWU	Transport and Industrial Workers' Union
TLL	Trinidad Leaseholds Limited
TLP	Trinidad Labour Party
UBOT	United British Oilfields of Trinidad

UDECOTT	Urban Development Corporation of Trinidad and Tobago
ULF	United Labour Front
UNC	United National Congress

Project Independence – After 56 Years

Introduction

This book grew out of a series of op-ed submissions to the local print media written between the 11th and 28th August 2018 in anticipation of the 56th anniversary of Independence of Trinidad and Tobago.

Not all the installments were published by the newspapers. Friends encouraged the author to put this together as a book.

So, the idea of this publication was born.

Though only 5 decades and a half have passed since August 31[st,] 1962, many of the developments in this short history of this twin-island country at the southern end of the Caribbean chain are not familiar to too large a segment of its population.

Despite the publication of several books on history, there is still much to be done to document the experience of the country and its post-colonial journey.

It is little wonder that the current Prime Minister has struck a chord with many with his call for the documentation and sharing of the nation's history.

Many fragments are unconnected or even unreported. Some only recorded in the interviews conducted by some with interests in particular aspects of the history with participants in events which have shaped the present realities. The oral record is disappearing as generations pass.

This is one attempt to examine this history from the perspective of the connection between events, people and circumstances since that day when "*a miniature state will be established, but a society and a nation will not have been formed*" as the country's first Prime Minister put it on the eve of Independence.

Project INDEPENDENCE and the nation-building project are the strivings of the people of this land to construct that society and nation for which they have sacrificed since the days of colonial imposition.

This publication is a contribution to the record of the experience of the project and offers some ideas for its continued pursuit and the realization of the hopes and aspirations of those who continue to work for its success.

Clyde Weatherhead
Port of Spain
April 2019

The Approaching Years & Context

As we approach the 56th Anniversary this month-end, we have the opportunity once more to reflect on **Project Independence** with the valuable experience of these years behind us.

I guess the fact that 1962 – the birth of our nation - was only 6 years before my own coming into this world provides me with the excuse or possibility of reflecting on the experience. For the elder ones, their reflections would certainly be more profound than mine could ever be.

Like with all worthwhile projects, it is useful to engage in evaluation at points along the timeline to see Where We Were, Where We Are and Where We Are Going.

Such evaluation would be most effective if we had Gantt Charts (Project Plans) which would have projected a critical path, the targets of which would be timed and measurable.

What we had at Day One, were more hopes, sentiments and expectations rather than a chartered course for the journey we set out on as a newly-independent nation on August 31, 1962.

A look back at what our circumstances were in the approaching years and the context – internal and international - which would have helped to shape those circumstances would be useful only if to remind us of Where We Were.

The Context of History

It is tempting to go all the way back to the point of European contact with our islands in 1492 to establish context. However, for the purposes of evaluating Project Independence, a more useful starting point may be what might be called the **Struggle for Independence** 1937 -1962.

That period began with the anti-colonial uprising popularly known as the Butler Riots. This anti-colonial struggle was spread across the nation and linked to similar events in other Caribbean territories.

It was both an economic and political battle which challenged the very foundations of the colonial imposition of the British Empire. Inscribed on its banner were 2 vital slogans – Let Those Who Labour Hold the Reins and the demand for Home Rule (the call for self-determination).

This Struggle for Independence, of course, was built on the experience of developments and movements of our people in the early years of the 20th Century, extending back to Emancipation.

Here are some mile markers in this important period:

> 1937 – 1939 – the Butler Riots and the legalisation of modern trade unions
> 1939 – 1945 – devastating World War, defeat of the Axis powers, strengthening of US global power, expansion of the Soviet Union and emergence of the Decolonisation Period
> The major boom in the local oil industry based on the importance of supply to the British war effort; the leasing of bases to the US on TT soil
> 1946 – first elections under universal suffrage and emergence of parties claiming to represent labour
> 1947 – Constitution Reform recommendations for an elected majority in the Colonial structures

of Governance; the emergence of even more political parties and independent candidates

➤ 1946 onward – the resumption of trade union organisation and industrial action starting with the release of union leaders from detention after the War

➤ 1955 – 62 the rise of the PNM with its first election victory with 39% of the vote in 1956, forming government with the First Chief Minister; the PDP (later DLP) won 20% of the vote. PNM shifted positions in an attempt to widen its political base by supporting strikes, the March on Chaguaramas in 1960, etc.

➤ 1958 – PNM and Williams in an effort to secure victory in the Federal Elections introduced racial hostility against the new DLP by suggesting that it represented a racial threat, even though it was a coalition of 3 parties. The DLP won 6 of the 10 seats.

➤ 1961 – Elections involve open racial tension and violence and a State of Emergency. The outcome – PNM won 20 seats and DLP 10 –

marking the establishment of the two-party system

➢ 1955 – 61 After economic growth at an average 10% per year, downturn in the economy began in 1961-62 as international oil prices began to fall

➢ 1960 – major strike in the oil industry and demand for nationalization of the industry.

On to Independence

With this background of emerging economic downturn, the rise of divisive racial tension in politics, cementing of 2-party political and electoral processes, growing strength and militancy of the trade union movement, Independence Day approached.

This was a development also encouraged by the rapidly successful Decolonisation Movement among the countries of Asia, Africa and Latin America which were gaining momentous victories in their struggles for an end to colonial rule.

The successes of Indian Independence (1947), the Chinese Revolution (1949), defeat of the French at

Dien Bien Phu in Viet Nam (1955), the convening of the Bandung Conference (1955) involving 29 newly independent Asian and African countries, the Cuban Revolution (1959), establishment of the Non-Aligned Movement (1961) – all of these provided more encouragement for countries seeking Independence and accelerated the demise of the British and other European Empires.

The emergence of Cold War and superpower rivalry for world hegemony was also a factor in the context of the situation as August 31, 1962 approached.

It was a complex historical moment, with both positive and negative aspects.

Internally, the demand for Home Rule, for Representative Government, for Nationalisation of the oil industry were all driving the demand for Independence.

However, the emergence of racially divisive politics between the Federal Elections in 1958 and the 1961 Elections, were a negative factor which was to influence the very negotiation of the Constitutional arrangements for Project Independence.

All these factors would also have a profound effect on the **nation-building project** that was to begin from Independence Day 1962.

Chapter 2 will examine the commencement of the nation-building project and some of the choices made in and after 1962 and their effect on Project Independence.

The Nation-Building Project - Choices

"31st of August 1962, I, a little dah-dah head boy stand on de by-pass, as colonial motorcade with de Queen face pass, on de by-pass. Forged from the love of liberty, but de country in de hands of the Yankee". These are the opening lines of a poem by Lancelot Doughty, a people's poet of San Fernando.

In his own way he records that day, the day when the Colonial "motorcade" passed. But there was a 'but'.

Did our two-island state really claim its sovereignty and break free of the web of a Plantation economy, a Crown Colony governance system and begin our path to development, building a society in favour of the people of Trinidad and Tobago?

"Massa day done!" was the cry. This was opportunity to embark on the nation-building project; our 'land's great dawning' as one of our earliest 'nation-building' songs proclaimed.

It was a heady time, a time of great expectations. It was a time for making choices, choices about the overall shape of the nation-building project – by whom and to what end. How to reshape the relationship between Tobago and Trinidad.

It was a time about making choices about the economy – how to build it, who to lead it, how to serve overall development, choices about the distribution of wealth.

Choices were to be made about governance – what kind of political and electoral systems, in whom or what is sovereignty to be vested.

The principal blueprint of the institutions of governance were decided at Marlborough House – the Independence Constitution. Who decided? The two-party political construct arbiters and the departing colonial power.

More choices: How to shape the culture, social relations, race relations, building our new nation and society.

Tackling the Nation-building Project

Right here, on our shores, other conversations were proceeding.

Organisations, other than the political parties, were discussing the shaping of the economy and a range of actions to be components of the Nation-building project. These represented, in today's terms, the non-governmental organisations' intervention.

There were organisations like **the New World Group** analyzing our Caribbean strategic economic options. Lloyd Best, Arthur Lewis and others were there.

There was also **Pegasus**, examining various elements of nation-building. This group was founded and led by Geddes Granger (later Makandal Daaga).

Both were formed in the year of Independence – 1962. The New World Group was more regional in its activity. Pegasus was TT-focused.

Not much is widely known about Pegasus and its contribution to our nation-building project. A detailed history of its work was presented by Roy Mitchell, its President, at a *Conference on the 20th Anniversary of the 1970 Revolution* at UWI St. Augustine in April 1990[1].

The work of Pegasus –

- Under its National Heroes Committee organised the first national awards on Independence Day, an upgrade of its Artists Awards.
- Organised National Debating Competitions among Secondary Schools and a Model United Nations
- Established "Project Independence" focusing on political, social, cultural and economic areas of national life
- Its National Sports Committee developed a proposal for a National Stadium for which the Trincity Development Company was going to donate land
- Its National Arts and Cultural Committee planned the establishment a National Arts Centre to be cited at the Princess Building Grounds in the capital

---

[1] Mitchell: all pages

- Its National Social Committee conducted studies in social development and worked for greater co-ordination of all existing social development agencies
- Project POS developed a plan for the rejuvenation of the capital city
- The structure of Pegasus included a broad cross-section of citizens, prominent and ordinary, organised in its branches across the country and in its various subject area committees.

This was the first major attempt by citizens to be involved in making decisions about the building and future of our society.

In the early years of Independence, all these initiatives of the people were usurped by the political directorate.

They were stalled, delayed or just never implemented. A National Stadium was built long after but in Port of Spain. The National Academy for the Performing Arts (NAPA) came much later and on the same site chosen by Pegasus. Port of Spain was never re-planned and has degenerated into a shameful excuse for a capital city.

The Direction for the Economy

The period between the end of World War II and 1962 was an important period for this country.

The oil industry which had major expansion due to the British military modernization and expansion in both World Wars became the main factor in the country's GDP and exports (up to 80% of foreign exchange earnings by 1960-61). By 1956 Texaco and UBOT/Shell dominated both oil production and refining.

Sugar and cocoa exports dominated the agriculture sector and by 1960 the Tate & Lyle monopoly was complete in the sugar industry. The expansion of world cocoa production saw the flavouring cocoas exported by this country losing market share.

A significant manufacturing sector was emerging. There were two influences – the need for goods to supply the US military bases during World War II and the adoption of the Puerto Rican-style 'industrialisation by invitation' strategy beginning in 1946-47.

Tourism development was also based on offering tax concessions and incentives. The Hotel Development Corporation was set up for hotel development in Tobago in 1957.

In Trinidad, oil and sugar exports and manufacturing predominated. In Tobago, only in the 1950's was there any significant development, largely due to the efforts of the island's sole Parliamentary representative, A.P.T. James. Electricity supply began in 1952, water production facilities from 1926 were expanded and a deep water harbour established at Scarborough.

Tobago exported large amounts of food crops in the decades up to the 1950's then declined as the CMA[2] marketing network was curtailed. Tourism development, started in the 1930's, expanded in the 1950's to become the major economic activity and source of employment on the island.

---

[2] Central Marketing Agency replaced by NAMDEVCO – National Agricultural Marketing and Development Company

The public sector after 1959 was becoming increasingly significant in promoting growth as Five-Year Plans were introduced in 1950.

While oil dominated exports, manufacturing failed to become an important foreign export earner. Importation of capital, foreign input goods and services increased. But, the growth areas in the economy created or maintained relatively few jobs.

Economic growth of 8-10% per annum in the 6 years leading to 1961 declined to 1% in 1962 as world oil prices plunged.

In these circumstances, the reliance on the oil industry, heavy foreign ownership in oil, sugar, banking and finance and manufacturing sectors, continuation of concessionary 'pioneer industry' policies in manufacturing and tourism, absence of comprehensive agricultural planning all continued at the start of project Independence in 1962.

Cultural Identity

The nation-building project needed not only an economic foundation, forging a cultural identity was a vital aspect.

In the context of the drive for 'home rule' and decolonization particularly after the Butler Riots of 1937, the forging of a new cultural identity began.

The work of those involved in the creative sectors – writers and artists in various fields – looked to the fledgling society for inspiration and contributed to national and world culture.

Beryl McBernie emerged in the 30's and 40's as a pioneer researching and promoting folk culture and African, Indian, French and Spanish cultural traditions, using the Little Carib Theatre as a vehicle.

The staunch defence by the people of the Shouter Baptists, calypso, steelband, oral traditions among the communities of people of African and Indian origin also contributed to creating the new cultural identity.

By 1962, Pegasus promoted the recognition of indigenous artists and cultural contributors with the introduction its Artistic and Cultural Awards as its first project, paying tribute to those excelling in all aspects of the arts and culture.

One internationally hailed author was moved to tears at the indigenous recognition paid to his work for the first time.

The hope for Project Independence was the flourishing of this new cultural identity and the possibility of forging the national personality.

Political Development

The demand for increased political participation by the majority of the society and dismantling of the Crown Colony system was interrupted by World War II.

Trade union activity was suppressed, and Butler and other leaders of the workers' movement were detained.

In 1946-7, in response to rising prices, low wages and unemployment, labour struggles exploded to again be suppressed under the **Emergency Powers**

Ordinance. The political powers promoted 'responsible' trade unionism in preference to 'Butlerism', sowing the seeds of division within the trade union movement.

The structures of power were adjusted as changes began in the 1940's. The numbers of elected officials versus nominated Unofficials in the Legislative Council was increased. In the Executive Council, the elected members were increased to 2 in 1941 and 4 in 1944.

The demand for expansion of the Right to Vote, led by the labour movement, finally succeeded in 1946 with the eligibility of all persons over 21 to exercise their franchise.

The attempts of the colonial authorities to limit universal adult suffrage using property and income qualifications and even ability to understand spoken English were defeated.

The era of mass electoral politics began with 46% of the population registered to vote. The number of political parties increased, and several independent candidates participated in the 1946 Elections.

By 1950, a Cabinet-like administrative system was introduced. In the elections of that year, though more seats (18) were contested and Butler's party became the largest single group in the legislature, they were excluded from the Executive Council. Instead, Albert Gomes was put in charge of the 'ministerial' regime by the colonial authorities.

By the 1956 Elections, 3 new parties were formed, the West Indian Independence Party (1952), the People's Democratic Party (1953) and the People's National Movement (1955). A Cabinet with a Chief Minister was now introduced.

The PNM won 13 seats, the PDP 5, the TLP, Butlerites and Independents won 2 seats each. The PNM formed the Government and Dr. Williams was Premier.

In 1957, the PDP, Trinidad Labour Party and Political Progress Group united to form the Democratic Labour Party.

In 1961, internal self-government with a bi-cameral legislature was in place and the PNM won the general elections with 20 of 30 seats. The DLP became the

Opposition. This marked the cementing of the 2-party system.

Like the concentration in the economy of monopolies in oil and sugar, in the political sphere between 1946 and 1961, the participation in electoral politics was concentrated from several parties and independents to just 2 main parties.

The hope for the Independence Project was for further democratization of the governance system and for real participation of the people in decision-making.

The choices made in 1962 in terms of the control of the nation-building project, the architecture of the government system and location of sovereignty, the continuation of the policy of 'industrialisation by invitation', the further development of the culture of the new nation were to determine the people's assessment of project Independence in the early years and their reaction to the effects of the choices made.

Those reactions will be examined in Chapter 3.

8 Years Later – Disappointment to Action

The mood of expectancy and hope that existed among the population when the Union Jack was lowered and the Red, White and Black hoisted outside the Red House at a minute past midnight on August 31, 1962 was pervasive.

With all the symbols of a newly-independent country – national flag, coat of arms and anthem, the streets of Port of Spain adorned with decorations and bunting and the singing of 'nation-building' songs, 'our nation was born'.

Beneath all the pomp and ceremony, however, certain realities persisted. Those realities would undermine the Independence euphoria as the population almost immediately began to face the realities of the new emerging nation state.

The choices made in moving to Independence, particularly, the choices of economic strategy, political culture and governance architecture began to impact the lives and livelihood of the expectant population, not in ways they were led to anticipate.

The euphoria of Independence was more a sigh of relief given the tensions generated in the political sphere between 1958 and the Marlborough Conference in May 1962.

The Atmosphere of Division

The genesis of threatening tensions was to be found in the consolidation of party politics and the 2-party system with the following developments:

- ➢ 1953 – formation of the PDP led by Bhadase Sagan Maraj who was a 3-in-1 leader – political party, trade union (ATSEFTWU) and religious organisation (Maha Sabha), guaranteeing him wide support for the PDP in the rural sugar belt.
- ➢ 1955 – formation of the PNM led by Dr. Eric Williams whose association with the teachers' group (TECA) and professionals in the Political Education Group (PEG) bolstered his appeal to an urban audience.

➢ 1956 – Elections postponed from 1955, PNM recognising the PDP as its strongest rival, adopted a strategy of portraying the PDP as a communal Hindu organisation. The outcome was PNM won the urban and suburban areas and the PDP remained strong in the rural areas. This geography expressed in demographic terms was the beginning of the notion of an 'African' PNM and 'Indian' PDP.

➢ 1958 - Federal Election. The DLP (an amalgamation of the PDP, TLP and POPPG a year earlier) won 6 of 10 seats defeating the PNM.

➢ 1961 - the General Elections, saw appeals to race become the strategy of both the PNM and DLP, now led by Capildeo. Political violence by PNM supporters against DLP meetings particularly in some areas of the East-West Corridor prompted a state of emergency, strangely imposed in several rural areas, causing a suspension of DLP outdoor meetings.

By 1962, the polarised and divisive politics based on appeals to race was threatening the unity of the population on the eve of Independence.

Winner Take All Governance Approach

The already edgy atmosphere worsened when the PNM took a unilateralist, non-bipartisan approach on major decisions on the country's future.

First, rather than seeking national consensus, the PNM party convention was used as the forum for a final decision on the issue of federation.

Second, the PNM Government decided to unilaterally draft the proposed independence Constitution with no consultation with the Opposition, only adding fuel to the atmosphere of division and tension.

The Queen's Hall Constitution Conference suggested limits on the Prime Minister's powers, Public and Judicial Service Commissions and room between the Senate and government. But most amendments were not agreed in the Parliamentary debate.

At the Independence Conference at Marlborough House in London, only at the last minute, in the atmosphere of racial and political polarisation back home, did the PNM accept several Constitutional positions advocated by the DLP, including, limiting the powers of the Executive by requiring consultation with the Opposition Leader on all major national appointments, requirement for special majorities to amend entrenched provisions, an independent Election and Boundaries Commission.

The PNM's preference for 'responsible' trade unionists also led to mounting tensions between it and Butlerite union leaderships which were gaining strength in and around 1962:

- The rebel leadership of George Weekes in the OWTU (1962)
- the creation of National Union of Sugar Workers challenging Bhadase in the ATSEFWTU (1963),
- the creation of Transport and Industrial Workers Union (TIWU) by bus workers leaving another union.

All of these were signs of the strengthening of the 'rebel' leaders and there was growing tension between them and the PNM, starting with the OWTU strike at Texaco, Apex and Shell in 1960.

These factors all contributed to the undercurrent of tension in the atmosphere of high expectations on August 31, 1962

The Experience of Independence

The fall in world oil prices in 1961-62 triggered a downturn in the economic fortunes of the country at the dawn of Independence. Government's fiscal deficit reached $56.4M in 1961.

This was one consequence of the economic strategy adopted by the Government even before Independence.

In the early independence years, several weaknesses of the economic choices became apparent:

- the offering of tax incentives to attract foreign capital left the state without sufficient resources to sustain economic development

- the manufacturing sector did not generate the expected increases in employment
- the drive for industrialisation led to neglect of agriculture
- the dependence on foreign industrial inputs and capital goods led to balance of payments problems.

In the course of the 1960's the economic outcomes had certain impacts on working and living conditions and social consequences for the population, for the workers in particular.

All the major commercial banks were foreign owned. So, was half of the land and 80% of manufacturing investment was by foreign capital. Most foreign investment was in oil.

There was a shift of the population from the rural to the urban parts of the country and out of agriculture.

Proportion of Population	1946	1960	1970
Living in rural areas	36.4%	23.3%	
Living in urban areas		40%	53%
Involved in agriculture and related activities	27.5%	21.1%	
Involved in mining and manufacturing	22.3%	22.5%	21%

The rates of unemployment and underemployment were increasing. Underemployment rose from 14.5% in 1960 to 20% in 1970. Income distribution was a constant and worsening problem. In the early 1960's the top 10% of income earners shared 33% of the national income. The wages for women were about 50% of those of their male counterparts.

A study in 1971 by Acton Camejo[3] revealed that unequal income distribution was closely linked with racial factors. The study showed that among executive and managerial staff in larger firms 53% were white,

[3] Camejo 1971: 301

15% were mixed, 9% Chinese, Indians 9% and Africans 4%.

The median monthly incomes, according to the 1960 census, for males was $500 for whites, $104 for Africans and $77 for Indians[4]. This pattern closely resembled the situation in the colonial era which was supposed to be the past. Industrial development was not delivering full or close to full employment and unequal distribution of income persisted.

By 1963, the unionised workers were on the move again. Strikes were being called by almost all the major unions in 1962 and 63. In February 1963, BP workers went on strike over the planned retrenchment of 200 workers. In October 1964, the unions boycotted Tripartite Committee talks.

In February 1965 sugar workers went on strike against a wage freeze imposed by the company. The strike was supported by the OWTU. At the same time, there were strikes at Lock Joint, Federation Chemicals and

---

[4] Kiely 1996: 109

even the CSA was threatening a go-slow over wage demands in the Civil Service.

A State of Emergency, using the 1947 Emergency Powers Ordinance, banned public meetings in the sugar belt to keep oil and sugar workers apart.

On March 18, 1965, Government released the report of the Mbanefo Commission which was set up in 1963 to investigate what government and some 'conservative' trade unionists called 'subversive political activity' in the trade union movement.

In just 48 hours, 18-20 March 1965, the Industrial Stabilisation Act was passed in Parliament and assented to by the Governor General. This law was principally aimed at restricting the workers right to strike. It banned strikes in 'essential services' – electricity, fire, health, water and sanitation. It introduced compulsory arbitration at the Ministry of Labour and in the Industrial Court.

Williams himself later declared that the ISA was aimed against "*the subversive elements in the society.*" and that the "*background was an open attempt to link the trade unions in oil and sugar*" (Eric Williams, **Inward Hunger**, p 311)

Williams blamed the unions for the low levels of capital investment and uncompetitive exports to justify this draconian law.

The fact was that the difficulties in the economy were a result of the development strategy of the Government itself as discussed above.

Five-year economic planning was abandoned.

The ambitious project to establish a port and industrial park at Point Lisas in Couva in 1966 initially did not make a difference. This port was a demand of the San Fernando businessmen who wanted access for their imports.

The passage of the ISA also achieved the further division of the trade union movement and split the Trade Union Congress, weakening the workers' fight for rights and interests, for jobs and incomes and for national control of the major economic enterprises.

In that same year, 1966, a new political party, the Workers and Farmers Party (WFP) came on the scene, attempting to break the stranglehold of the now established 2-party control. The major parties, by their combined strategy, accused the WFP of offering 'dictatorship' and defeated it.

All the declarations of 'Massa Day Done' and the euphoria of Independence were turning into disappointment at the failure of the promise of Independence. The disappointment was acutely felt among the urban youth who, despite expanded educational opportunities, were unemployed and without employment prospects in increasing numbers.

1970 – The Revo – Disappointment to Action

By the end of the 60's the attempts by Pegasus to create a people's programme for nation-building were frustrated and usurped by the Government. Granger went on to the UWI campus and into the communities to begin a new phase of his struggle for development.

The workers and their unions were fighting battles to save jobs as employment in oil fell by 3% between 1965 and 1969. Automation in sugar led to retrenchment and in other sectors job cuts were the order of the day.

In June 1968, 10,000 workers joined in a March of Resistance. TIWU led the challenge against the ISA with strikes at Sissons Paints in 1967 and in public transport in June 1968 and the May 1969 Bus strike.

The disaffected among the unemployed and the intelligentsia at UWI were also in action. Some lecturers were challenging the thinking and policies of the Government. The university students engaged in protests on 26 February 1969 in support of 11 Trinidadian students arrested at Sir George Williams University in Canada.

The students also linked with the youth in the communities.

All these currents fed into what erupted on 26 February as the 1970 Revolution led by NJAC which was formed that night by students, youth, workers and their unions.

In 1970, mainly young persons, disillusioned with the persistence of the colonial construct, sought to address social inequality, foreign domination of the economy, racial inequality and poor political representation.

The shouts of '**Power to the People**' and sound of marching feet filled the air. The clarion call "**Indians and Africans, Unite!**" urging unity of the People, was inscribed on the banner. The youth re-examined history seeking a better understanding and appreciation of the society and its people and to define project independence anew.

The response of the 'independence' state was a mixture of ignoring ideas for a new development approach, offering a minimum of concessions, State of Emergency, imprisonment of leaders and brutal repression including the attempted dreaded Public Order Bill.

Like the colonial authorities' response to the Butler Riots, the approach to the 1970 Revo was 'Smiles and Blood' – token concessions and severe repression. Against those who dared resort to arms, the answer was blood and steel.

Against the adherence of the youth to revolutionary ideas of change, a new element was introduced to the society - the mass culture of illicit drugs.

A series of "Woodstock" events became an outlet for promoting narcotic drug use.

Understanding why, in less than a decade, the euphoria of Independence gave way to mass disillusionment, was not important. Protecting the new order of power was.

But, the idea of the new Trinbago remained alive among the workers and youth who dared to take action in 1970.

In the next Chapter, we examine the pattern of boom and bust in an unsustainable economic construct.

Windfall and Wastage – Saga of Unsustainable Economy

When the NJAC leaders were rounded up in the early hours of April 21, 1970 as another State of Emergency (SoE) was declared and the army mutiny that morning was diffused, the Government thought that the conflagration was doused.

However, into 1973-74, the embers of disaffection continued to smolder. The strikes and labour unrest persisted and armed fighters persevered despite police crackdown.

In 1971, strikes at FedChem and Dunlop supported by close to 4000 oil workers raged. Strikes at Texaco, Badger and Wimpey involved more than 1,000 workers. All of these were led by the OWTU.

Workers on the port, at TelCo and WASA wanted to join the OWTU and abandon the 'responsible' unions (which supported the ISA) in preference for the 'radical' 'Butlerite' unions.

Government's response – Declaration of another State of Emergency in October 1971, banning public meetings, detention of 10 leaders and replacement of the ISA by the Industrial Relations Act (IRA) introduced in Parliament almost simultaneously with the SoE.

The price control provision in the ISA (never implemented) was repealed and to stop the spread of 'radical' unions a prohibition of representation of more than one "essential industry" by a single union was added. This prompted another split in the trade union movement into the Labour Congress and Council of Progressive Trade Unions (CPTU).

Unrest persisted into 1973 and PM Williams threatened to resign encouraging the refrain of 'Don't go, Doctor. Don't go.'.

Dramatically, a development completely outside of this country's control occurred. There was a sharp increase in world oil prices, triggered by the Arab oil embargo, spawning yet another boom for this oil-exporting country.

In both World Wars, because of the needs of the British military, TT oil experienced booms.

In the late 50's, driven by the demands of the US market, the extension of marine drilling and refinery expansion out of Texaco's acquisition of TLL's assets, saw another boom in production to 70,000 bpd of oil and refinery throughput of 345,000 bpd by 1965.

The oil windfall of 1974-78 was the first based solely on increased oil prices. Oil prices which were declining between 1960-70, multiplied by 7 between 1972-78. Government's revenue rose from $591M TT in 1973 to TT1,398M in 1974 to $3,226M in 1978. Oil revenues increased 48 times by 1980 compared to 1972.

The balance of trade moved from -$360M TT in 1972 to +$340M in 1974 and +$1B in 1977.

On Independence Day 1974, Williams declared:

*"In our case oil means (a) a large number of permanent jobs through downstream petroleum operations or **new industries based on petroleum**, (b) greater national ownership of our national resources....and local*

*utilization and **diversification** of products which we formerly exported, (c) larger allocations for our domestic services, (d) more rapid progress....to supplement our own domestic efforts at **greater self-sufficiency**.*" (emphasis mine)

TT was floating on oil dollars.

YEAR	1951	1960	1970	1972	1973	1974	1977	1980
GDP ($M)	308.3	865.9	1630.9	2039.4	2554.7	4101.5	8552.2	14081.9

Government employment increased by hiring 100,000 people – 80,000 in the public service and 20,000 in partly government-owned commercial and industrial enterprises.

Oil windfall dollars were spent on increases in subsidies in food, welfare, utilities and petroleum, cuts in income and other taxes, employment creation, expanding state ownership in Texaco and Tate & Lyle and new joint ventures. This was the explosion in the state-owned enterprise (SOE) sector.

Despite the oil money, poverty and poor income distribution persisted.

Dissatisfaction Continues

In 1974-75, industrial unrest flared up again.

By March 1975, 17,000 sugar workers were on strike, cane farmers launched 'don't cut' campaigns, mass meetings in oil and protests at Neal & Massy and in other industries were escalating.

A rally and march were planned for March 18. More than 15,000 workers were on the move. The police refused permission for the march and brutally attacked in San Fernando, arresting 32 leaders of the ULF (a grouping of 4 unions). Police blocked the roads and overturned huge pots of food prepared for the marchers in Marabella and Saith Park, Chaguanas. That day became known as 'Bloody Tuesday'.

Within 6 days, the ULF converted into a political party dubbed a working-class party. The ULF had support from workers mostly in the 'radical' unions and organised among the university lecturers and students.

It contested the 1976 General Elections in September of that year.

The outcome of the election was: PNM won 24 seats, ULF – 10 and the DAC (led by A N R Robinson who left the PNM in 1971) – 2 Tobago seats.

Despite the large protests and strikes, the ULF failed to gain most of the working-class support. By September 1977, it had split into 2 factions, one led by Basdeo Panday, who enjoyed the support of the workers and people in the sugar belt.

The demands for unity of 1970 appeared to be silenced and the old pre-Independence pattern of politics based on appeals to race and division among the people seemed to be back.

Because of an opposition elections boycott, the PNM formed a minority (33%) government in 1971.

Largely because of the lavish spending of the oil windfall dollars, it was able to regain support by 1976.

The expansion of the industrial plants at Point Lisas using the expanding gas production locally was decided at a 1975 Conference on the best us of energy resources.

But, by the early years of the next decade, windfall turned into downturn very much as the situation was at the approach to Independence in 1962 and again at the start of the '70's.

The economy was like a roller coaster ride and the boom and bust pattern closely followed the pattern of prices for the main commodity on which the country relied – oil.

This pattern has not been broken since and sustainable economic development without the attendant regularity of crises is still to be achieved.

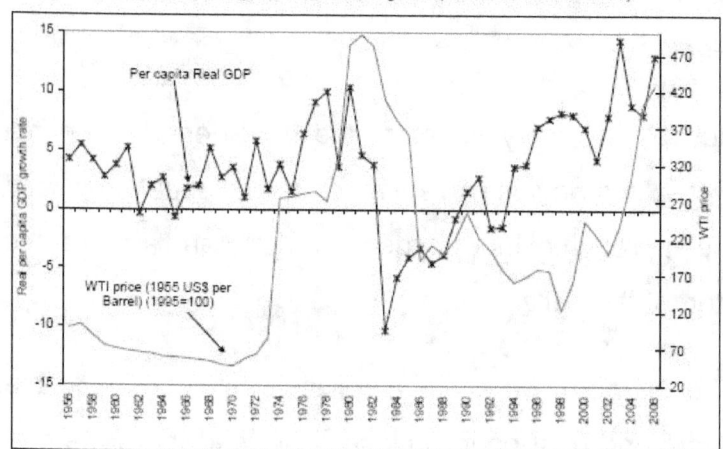

Figure 1. Percentage change real GDP per capita,
in constant US$ prices, and WTI price (in constant 1955 US$)

Source: T&T: Economic Growth in a Dual Economy, IDB, 2007

Into Recession Again - 1982

While oil prices 'bumped up' in 73-74 and again in 79-80, by 1985-86 they were halved.

By 1980, oil business amounted to 42% of GDP, provided 65% of government revenues and accounted for 94% of export earnings. Dependence on oil was a benefit and a threat.

Partly because of falling US demand for imported oil as refineries there stepped up production in response to the 1973 'oil crisis', both oil production and refinery throughput were on the decline in TT from around 1978.

The oil windfall, while it created the opportunity for government and the private sector to diversify, did not result in moving toward a less oil-dependent sustainable economy.

Government concentrated on very expensive economic projects with less-than-expected returns like ISCOTT, in the iron and steel sector.

Construction of the iron and steel complex started in 1977.

Several other gas-based plants were added to the Point Lisas estate with the establishment of the National Energy Corporation.

Most of the new industrial plants were owned by multinationals.

The local private sector preferred the comfort of retail operations and 'screwdriver' industries with high import content like the multiple car agencies and assembly plants.

Corruption assumed massive proportions. The bus station racket and Caura Dam scandal of Gene Miles' days paled in comparison to the new wave of feeding off the state trough which has persisted.

Between 1982 and 1989, there were 7 years of negative growth in GDP (more than enough to satisfy any definition of recession). GDP was $6229M US in 1984 and dropped to $5610M US in 1987. The burden of debt reached $1.41B US in 1987 and external debt servicing/GDP escalated from 2% in 1982 to 24.3% in 1987.

The1981 Chambers government devalued the currency by 50% in 1985 and added a 10% tax on some consumer goods.

The 1986 NAR government rode in on a wave of 'one love' and a massive 33-3 majority and continued Chambers' "adjustment" measures:

- ❖ 1987 – suspension of COLA for public employees, plan to retrench 7000 sugar workers. A plan to retrench hundreds of public officers was thwarted when the unions exposed this decision contained in a Cabinet Minute.

- ❖ 1988 – second devaluation of TT dollar, 5% 'mobilisation' tax both led to increased prices for basic goods. In July, Government refused to implement a pay increase ordered by the industrial court, announcement in Budget of intention to go to the IMF and first IMF loan
- ❖ 1989 – 2nd IMF loan, 10% pay cut for public employees
- ❖ 1990 – introduction of VAT at 15%

The 'austerity' programme of the NAR included mass retrenchment - more than 30,000 construction workers, 8,000 jobless on closure of DEWD in 1987, attrition among public officers and daily-paid government workers. Unemployment rose from 10% in 1981 to 18% in 1986 and 23% by the end of the 80's.

A huge debt of over $2B was owed to over 100,000 public sector employees resulting from the pay cuts which were ruled illegal by the Courts.

Unemployment, poverty, vagrancy and vending spread all over the country.

The Kirpalani[5] conglomerate collapsed in 1986 and bankruptcies dealt with many other private companies.

The savagery of the attack on the workers and poor to ensure the 'inescapable obligation' of debt payments drove the divided trade union movement to act together against the state and private sector assault.

Neal & Massy froze wages, cut work time and contracted out work. That conglomerate locked out workers at its subsidiaries – Polymer Caribbean, Edgar Borde, Electrical Industries, Automotive Components and N&M Motors. Unions rallied with TIWU which bore the brunt of these attacks.

March 6, 1989 was declared a **Day of Resistance** – a massive one-day national strike, led by the Joint Trade Union Movement (JTUM). It was followed by strikes in oil and at PTSC and WASA, among others.

The 1990 Budget and 15% VAT drove the unions to expand the coalition of resistance in a single labour day march that year and the creation of the Summit of

---

[5] One of the first local mega-businesses. The Neal &Massy and Ansa-McAl groups of companies later became large conglomerates.

People's Organisations (SOPO). Eventually, a new single trade union federation, the National Trade Union Centre, NATUC, was created when the PSA Rooftop Accord was signed in 1991.

The NAR disintegrated in 1988 when Basdeo Panday and some Ministers supporting him were fired by PM Robinson.

They formed Club 88 and founded the UNC in April 1989.

By 1990, the NAR which began with 'One Love' was facing unceasing social unrest and eventually on July 27, the Jamaat al Muslimeen attempted to overthrow it in an unsuccessful coup.

The oil windfalls passed through the society 'like a dose of salts' and TT marched into the 'valley of debt'.

Heading Where?

The economic strategy adopted before, continued at Independence, persisted in through 2 major windfalls in the 70's and 80's left Project Independence floundering and the nation-building project in tatters.

The shift in dependency from liquid to gaseous hydrocarbons did nothing to free the economy and the country from the single-commodity 'plantation' economic construct inherited from colonial times.

The structure of the economy never changed, and the diversification promised by Williams on Independence Day 1974 and other PMs since then has never materialized.

Agriculture has been annihilated and the persistently mounting food import bill stands testimony to an undeveloped subsistence sector despite the various Oil and Food Conferences and plans touted over the years.

The tourism sector has never contributed as much as 10% of GDP and the economy rises and falls as global hydrocarbon prices fluctuate. Inconsistent exploration and production efforts also hampered the economics of the dominant energy sector.

The dependence on foreign capital and the US gas market after its oil market collapsed left project Independence without the economic base for success and recurring crises of boom and bust up to the 2014-18 recession accompanied by huge deficit-financing and mounting public debt and debt payment issues.

The governance remains the maximum leader PM and Cabinet dictatorship patterned on the Colonial Governor-ship as the demand for 'Power to the People' raised in the call for Home Rule in the 30's and 40's and rekindled in 1970 remains a hope and prospect yet to be realized.

The SOE's in the economy and SoE's in suppressive rule every time the people demand a new way continue are used to suffocate the advance of the nation-building project and Project Independence.

In Chapter 5, we look at the state of things at the jubilee celebration of the 50th anniversary in 2012.

At the Golden Jubilee

The decade of the 90's was one of 'recovery' in many ways. It opened with the signing of a structural adjustment loan with the World Bank, probably the last major act of the NAR government. The NAR departed the political scene and the PNM and UNC took turns in office.

Even our Olympic experience in that decade was less than scintillating. Nineteen athletes journeyed to 2 Olympiads and the medal return was 2 bronze medals, both won by a single athlete, Ato Boldon.

The currency had a 'fixed' float and exchange controls were removed as the full liberalization package was implemented, mostly for the benefit of local manufacturers in the export trade. Electricity generation was divested and after a couple bouts of voluntary separation, Severn Trent was brought into WASA. Privatisation was on the way.

Structural adjustment continued to have negative social effects. Unemployment remained between 20 and 10%. Public sector workers persisted in their fight to recover the $2+B debt owed by the state, created by the pay, increment and COLA cuts in the late 80's.

One Minister claimed that the 'structure' of the economy changed as the energy industry switched from oil to gas, hydrocarbon all the same. The economy was still described as 'energy-based' as hydrocarbons still accounted for 87% of exports, 48% of government revenue and 43% of GDP, while providing only 4% of all employment.

Gas plants were littering the landscape at Point Lisas and Point Fortin in a caravan of 'trains'. Once again, the multinationals claimed the lion's share and markets on the Eastern seaboard of the US were the primary destination. Not long after the end of the decade, there were 9 ammonia plants in operation.

After the windfalls in 1972-73, and in 1980-81 - boosted by the misfortune of others (the Iran-Iraq war), oil prices steadily declined in the 90's to a low of $10 per barrel in 1998.

Oil production steadily dropped from a peak of 230,000 barrels per day (bpd) in 1978 to about half of that just after the turn of the century. Gas production rose sharply and flattened at 4.1B cubic feet per day in the first 7 years of the next decade.

Into the 21st Century

As the new millennium began, the recovery from the 80's recession was ending. The government touted TT as a success story of structural adjustment. GDP was improving mostly because of the gas 'bubble'.

While the economy was showing positive signs, in the area of governance a new crisis emerged. The stain of withdrawal from international Human Rights bodies to facilitate hangings in 1999 continued to taint the nation's reputation internationally.

The UNC retained office in the December 11, 2000 General Elections, but questions about the fairness of the elections persisted. Within one year the UNC was split and the administration collapsed in office amid corruption allegations.

Elections were called again in December 2001 and for the first time in the electoral history since 1956, there was a tie - 18-18. President Robinson using euphemisms about *"streams into rivers"*, appointed PNM Leader, Patrick Manning, as PM based on *'moral and spiritual values'*, rather than Constitutional convention.

For 10 days or so, the country was run by its civil servants, with no Cabinet in place.

For the third time in 2 years, Elections were called on October 7, 2002. The PNM won 20 of the 36 seats. There was a series of issues including the adoption of the CCJ as final Court of Appeal on which the politicians flip-flopped as Parliament continued to be tied up in squabbles and corruption charges aimed at both sides of the aisle.

In 2003, crime, which had been escalating since the mid-90's, exploded with a rash of over 150 kidnappings and the murder toll reached 166.

Panday was on 3 charges for integrity violations of non-disclosure of a London bank account.

In mid-year, utilising a 1995 loan agreement with the IADB, negotiated in a period spanning PNM and UNC governments, Caroni Ltd was closed down putting 8,000 sugar workers out of work.

Later in the year, PM Manning announced a major Cabinet reshuffle in which 15 Ministers and junior Ministers were affected. The political unease continued and in 2005, the number of seats in the Lower House was increased to 41 to try and avoid recurrence of an electoral tie.

The crime scourge grabbed further attention when 13 people were injured in a bomb explosion on Frederick Street, downtown Port of Spain.

10,000 people joined a 'Death March' protesting the failure of government to deal with the escalating violent crime situation.

In 2007, General Elections were called in November. The PNM, UNC and Congress of the People, COP formed in 2006, contested, and the PNM won 26 seats, failing to attain the special majority that Manning was looking for.

After drafting a Constitution to further concentrate power in the hands of a President and limit checks and balances on such maximum power, government also introduced an unpopular new Property Tax in 2009 while allegations of corruption connected with the construction projects managed by UDECOTT continued unabated.

Many warned that Government's mega-project construction drive might 'overheat' the economy.

For the second time, in 2010, PM Manning called early elections and a coalition of opposition forces, the People's Partnership, was formed. The PP defeated the PNM, 29 seats to 12, and the first female Prime Minister Kamla Persad Bissessar headed the new government.

A Third 'Oil' Windfall?

In the first 7 years of the new millennium, natural gas production increased at an average compounded rate of about 13% per year. Natural gas prices rose at an average compounded rate of 17% and methanol and ammonia prices 11 and 13% per year, respectively. Oil prices, too, dramatically rose from $28.1US to $94.1US per barrel between 2003-2008. Crude oil production rose to a maximum of close to 55,000 bpd in 2006-7. Natural gas production rose steadily until about 2010.

Real GDP increased steadily because of the energy ('oil') sector situation up to 2010, the new 'windfall' cushioning the effect of the global financial crisis.

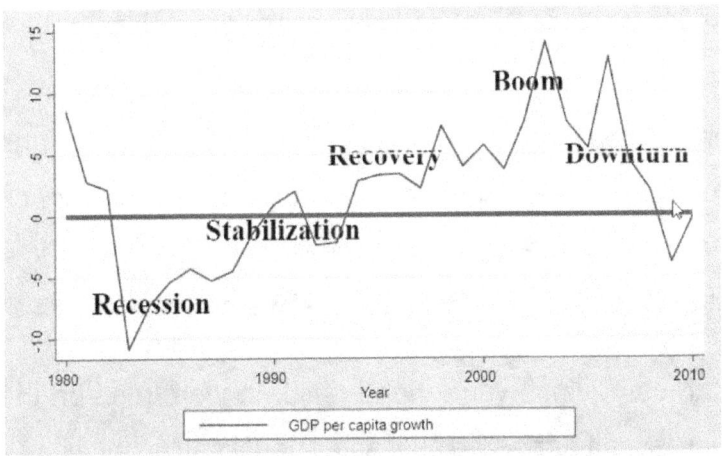

SOURCE: ISER presentation on Natural Resource Curse and Socio-economic Dilemma

The economy was booming as we approached the golden jubilee of project Independence in 2012.

While the situation was buoyant and government spending on the increase, the gas 'bubble' was in danger of bursting as gas production was heading for decline in the absence of new arrangements to encourage new drilling.

The daily body count escalated as the murderous spree of violent crime remain largely unchecked. The annual toll peaked at 550 in 2008, 509 in 2009 and 485 in 2010 and by 2012 had returned to the same level as in 2005.

3,858 citizens had been slaughtered since 2000.

There seemed to be no solution, as detection and conviction rates reached abysmal levels. The violence was being fueled by the drug and gun trade and attendant gang violence and turf wars.

Crimes against women and children were also on the increase. It appeared as if a new level social decay was gnawing away at the very fabric of the society and undermining the nation-building project.

The 50th anniversary of Independence was being marked with pomp and ceremony reminiscent of the euphoria of 1962. The lavish bunting on the waterfront (itself a product of the third energy windfall) and around the capital, the re-enactment of the replacement of the

Union Jack by the Red, White and Black in the first minutes of the 31st – these were reminders of hope and expectation that had dissipated in the course of 5 decades.

Government publications in tribute to a "**Terrific and Tranquil**" nation and hailing its "**Icons**", the sponsoring of a commemorative music CD and other events sought to convince an uneasy and anxious population that all was well with project Independence.

It was as if a government led by 'the other' party was trying perhaps too hard to convince that nation-building was on track even while, the 5th deficit budget amid growing GDP was in place and safety and security were becoming endangered.

Amid the celebratory atmosphere, President Maxwell Richards delivered a sobering message at the re-enactment ceremony. **T&T Not a Nation of Sheep** was the title of his speech in which he said:

"Tonight's event generates excitement, as it should. The occasion is as solemn, as it is pulsating. But

euphoria must not be allowed to cloud sober reflection, as reality will not go away.

We need to ask ourselves whether we are living up to the expectations of our freedom fighters, who did battle, not with guns, but with intellectual prowess, artisan skills, artistic brilliance, sport and diplomatic savoir faire to secure our place among the family of independent Nations."

"We speak of constitutional reform, for example, but that is in stasis.

"We made a promise to Tobago, a long time ago and, as Eric Williams said in Parliament with the joining of our two islands, administratively, one form of neglect was exchanged for another.

This is one of the major areas of brokenness that we can fix and must fix, if we are to proceed with dignity and vigour, in unity, over the next 50 years. Unity in diversity is only one, though very important, aspect of our national character.".

The President appealed for focus on the need to modernise our supreme law, the Constitution, which was created in an atmosphere of tension fostered by the threat of harmful disunity, to make it capable of fulfilling the promise of nationhood and meet the needs of the time.

He pointed to *'areas of brokenness'* - the unresolved issue of the relationship between Tobago and Trinidad in a nation in which we proclaim, 'side by side, we stand' and 'every creed and race find an equal place' in our national anthem which hailed our land's 'great dawning'.

Without resolving the relationship between our two islands and without ensuring the progress of the entire nation based on the unity of all of its people, nation-building and project Independence remain aspiration rather than reality.

After 50 years, our economy is still dependent on a single commodity, much as it was on sugar at the time of its birth.

Foreign investors and business interests still predominate in that critical sector and otherwise.

In 1962, we were assured 'Massa day done', yet at 50, we are not fully in control of our economic fortunes and able to satisfy the demands of guaranteeing the basic rights of our citizenry.

The alienation of the majority of the population from decision-making which affects their very lives and the future of the nation-building project has deepened as the attempts to concentrate even more power at the top as in the recent Constitutional amendment process in 2009-10 signalled.

In 1970, the cry was for 'power to the people', yet at 50, decision-making is within a circle of leadership in a governance construct that has not moved far from the fundamentals of the Crown Colony governorship, with claims of right of rulership and privileges of the governing over the governed.

At 50, amid apparent material abundance (defined by things), attention must be paid to the appeal of the President for all to pay attention to *"areas of brokenness that we can fix and must fix, if we are to proceed with dignity and vigour, in unity, over the next 50 years"*.

The tasks of nation-building and project Independence demand no less.

In chapter 6, we shall examine our Present and Future and the requirements of realising the aspirations of the 31st of August 1962.

Present and Future

As August 31st approaches, TT experienced a 'wake up' call on the 10th day before the anniversary of the launch of project Independence – the most powerful earthquake in living memory reminded us (if only temporarily) of the vulnerability of our existence and fragility of our 'material abundance'.

Already challenged by another devastating episode of economic collapse, having experienced the drama of a tortuous and incredulous selection process for a top cop created by Parliamentary unanimity in 2006, cringing at each murderous act of barbarity attempting to qualify as more horrendous than the last, we approach the end of the 56th year since 'our nation is born, leh meh tell yuh'.

Our Present

We are now 6 years beyond the golden jubilee of project Independence.

Since the 50th anniversary, some important developments have occurred:

- The 'gas bubble' did burst and new incentives offered to the energy barons in 2013 began to 'encourage' new gas production.

- In 2013, Local Government Elections were held with a Proportional Representation component for the appointment of Aldermen.

- In 2014, energy prices (oil and gas) did plummet once again putting our 'energy-dependent' economy into a tailspin, into a new round of recession about which the politicians flip flopped on either side of the 2015 General Elections.

- 2014 – the PP took a Constitution Amendment Bill to Parliament, after a very extensive consultation process begun in 2013. The Bill which would have established the Right of Recall of MP's by Electors, Fixed Terms for the PM and Fixed Election Dates, failed because of the inclusion of a Run-off provision and a vote against by Government members who campaigned for the first 3 changes since 2006.

- 2015 – General Elections saw the return of the PNM after a third 5-year interruption in its occupation of the position of Party-in-Power for 41 of the 56 years since 1962.

On the eve of August 31st:

> ➤ The country is borrowing (by loans, bonds, etc.) its way out of Recession (the most serious challenge in its history, some say)

> ➤ The Head of the Judiciary has just lost a legal battle at the Privy Council in his attempt to prevent the Law Association from investigating several allegations of inappropriate conduct on his part

> ➤ The ferry promised in November 2017 is ready for trial on the sea bridge, but officials warn that cars may not be accommodated because a protective canopy against sea blast is not yet installed

> ➤ The murder toll has crossed 360 by the 240th day of 2018 with another multiple murder recorded

> ➤ Unpreparedness for natural disasters though sitting in hurricane and earthquake zones, was

again highlighted by a rumble at 6.9 on the Richter scale

➤ The Leader of the longest-governing political party acknowledged his ignorance of the beliefs and culture of a significant sector of the multi-ethnic, multi-religious and multi-cultural society of which we boast

➤ Headlines screaming 'D-Day for Petrotrin' and 'Uneasy Times' heralded announcement of a plan to cease refinery operations after 104 years is made to unions and the country

➤ One 'major' political party's biggest Independence event was held in Tampa, Florida and the other will turn the sod for its new headquarters on August 30.

The mood in the country is of anxiety, concern for the future, fear, rather than celebration and anticipation usual at Independence time.

Already, the radio ads encourage us to '56 Love' and one TV ad depicts the physical infrastructure and legacy projects, 'nation-building' songs are added to radio playlists all in attempt to generate some enthusiasm for "happy Independence".

What we need to ask is: What is the state of our nation-building project?

The Nation-building Project

The words of the first Prime Minister in a message ahead of the first Independence Day reminds us that the nation-building project is what we are fundamentally engaged in:

"*On August 31, 1962, a country will be free, a miniature state will be established, but a society and a nation will not have been formed. After August 31, 1962, the people of Trinidad and Tobago will face the fiercest test in their history - whether they can invest with flesh and blood the bare skeleton of their National Anthem, 'Here, every creed and race find an equal place.'* – Dr. Eric Williams, **History of the People of Trinidad and Tobago**, page 282.

Perhaps, we may derive some assistance from these words of the current Project Manager (PM):

"*But we still have much work to do. As a nation, we have not yet realized the full measure of our promise.*"

– Dr Keith Rowley, Speech at **Dr. Eric Williams – 34 Years Later**, 2015

And what is the 'measure' of our progress?

Do we focus on how many Heads of Government we have had, as Nigeria did at the end of its 56th year, 2 years ago, under its 13th President, and its journey described as a *'tortuous road to nationhood'*?

Do we tally GDP figures or other economic indicators and ignore the current state of our economy or what has led to a decision to close our oil refinery after 104 years? Or without rethinking the fundamentals of an approach to economic development continued since the 1940's?

Do we count infrastructural projects, buildings, roads, bridges, 'legacy' structures while ignoring the fact that after 56 years it could be admitted after a potentially dangerous earthquake that we do not yet have an enforceable building code?

Do we count the number of vehicles on our roads while ignoring the absence of a reliable and efficient mass transit system since the abandonment of our railway and the rise and fall of the motor car assembly industry?

Do we evaluate our progress based on 'material abundance' based on the abundance of goods produced and available for consumption by various groups of society we label 'income groups'?

We have been encouraged to use these measures from the standpoint of objects and the products of the consumption industry. We promote the notion of consumption without even paying attention to how many people are employed in the production of basic things that we need - like food, clothing, housing as against how many are engaged in producing consumer items.

We even ignore how many are unemployed or being put out of employment and unable to have the means to obtain the necessities.

There is another view of 'material abundance' which focuses on people, rather than objects. This definition focuses on development of human resources and the encouragement of human initiative and human energy for the building of the nation.

In 1962, with the advent of Independence, motivated by the expectation of control of our society and development, scores of people in Pegasus and other organisations, their human initiative released, embarked on the nation-building project. There was such enthusiasm to contribute.

The irony was that the first PM and his government, strangled that initiative and energy since the people had no resources or control to be able to fully implement the projects they had conceived and developed.

The *'material abundance'* as objects and consumption replaced that as human development.

Without rebuilding real hope in the future as happened with the arrival of 'self-determination' in 1962, the *'full measure of our promise'* will never be realized.

Conflicting Interests

It is interesting that on this eve of the 56th anniversary one trade union is trying to convince Government to allow one set or businessmen to get control of the steel mill from which the workers were thrown out of jobs when the previous owners closed it down because they were not making enough profit.

The union is convinced that new owners will ensure their jobs. But their own recent experience shows that the employer and the employees each have interests of their own; the owner in maximum profit and the worker in keeping his job.

There are conflicting interests even when there may be seemingly common interests. The owner and the worker may seem to have a common interest in keeping the factory open, but each has their own interest.

Similarly, the banker and borrower also do not have the same interests.

Likewise, all politicians have one thing in common – they all want power. But, those in Government want to stay in power, while the Opposition have their own plans to come to power. They all promise they will solve the problems and the people should either put them or keep them in power to do so.

The people's experience shows them that there is a conflict between what they want and what the politicians want. There is even a conflict between what the politicians say and what they do.

So, each set of politicians promises to solve crime, to end corruption, to unite the people. They all promise 'change'.

But, after 56 years, the society is polarized because of party support and every effort to keep the people apart using race or religion is being made. Crime is rampant, corruption is denying the society of vital resources and is unpunished, the economy is in crisis, institutions are in a mess and degeneration and decay is destroying the very social order.

Even the problem, the 'area of brokenness' – the relationship between Tobago and Trinidad remains unsolved. There is before the Parliament a Bill for self-government for Tobago, proposed by a political party which opposed the idea when it was first raised by Robinson and Murray in 1977. This Bill is not satisfactory to the people of Tobago. Its content is little known by the people of Trinidad.

The Future

In four years, we will be marking the Diamond Jubilee, 60 years of Independence and the nation-building project, what will our assessment be then?

We cannot, at that or any other time in the future merely continue with hopes, sentiments and expectations. Nor can we continue with "constitutional reform, …. that is in stasis" as President Richards told us at the 50th anniversary, or an economy that is not diversified as promised by Dr Williams on Independence Day 1974.

We cannot continue with promises unfulfilled and a society under anti-social pressure and a nation…still not formed as we were urged even before August 31[st,] 1962.

The people must once again take charge of the nation-building project and project Independence and unleash their human energy with a plan and action if the nation envisaged in 1962 and named by the people in 1970 is to be realized – *Trinbago*.

Toward a Plan to Advance Project Independence

Project Independence was the title of an ambitious programme conceived by the founder of PEGASUS, Geddes Granger.

Its aim was to bring "all the talented forces in the country" to create a plan "to convert the 'unity of spirit'.... Into a new and dynamic 'unity of purpose'. It "identified the four most critical areas of national life, the political, the social, cultural and economic", as Roy Mitchell, then Pegasus Chairman put it.

The introductory paper of Project Independence declared: *"National purpose must precede and influence sectional interests, and this alone will lead to resolute endeavour on the part of all individuals and groups to work for the general welfare, development and happiness of the whole nation of Trinidad and Tobago".*[6]

Whether it was the demand that Those Who Labour

---

[6] Text of Paper at 20th Anniversary Conference on the 1970 Revolution, Roy Mitchell p. 8

Must Hold the Reins of Power or for Home Rule raised in 1937, or in the call for Power to the People shouted loudly in 1970, the desire of the people of this land has always been for the opportunity of All to Participate in the work to decide and implement policies, plans and programmes that 'benefit of the whole nation'.

Put another way, ensuring the well-being of All is a principle and goal of Democracy, properly understood.

The **Project INDEPENDENCE** that the nation embarked on 31st August 1962, as so well put by Pegasus, is precisely to ensure that everyone can contribute to ensuring the well-being of All.

But, this goal of the nation-building project has been set aside, dislodged and derailed precisely because "sectional interests" have dominated the national purpose.

The centre-stage of political affairs has been occupied, not by the people, but by others. The political actors who have claimed that space do not represent the national interest – the interest of the people and the well-being of All. They represent the interests and well-being of a small and shrinking minority.

To advance Project INDEPENDENCE and the nation-building project, the People must capture the centre-stage of politics once more in order to ensure that they establish the goal of ensuring the well-being of All.

The People have occupied the centre-stage of politics before; in 1937, 1970 and other moments in our history. They must do so once more to ensure the future of the whole nation of Trinidad and Tobago.

In the four critical areas of national life identified by Pegasus – political, economic, social and cultural – steps must be taken to ensure the future of the nation-building project.

Here are some proposed objectives in these critical areas to create a **Trinbago for the 21ˢᵗ Century**:

❖ **POLITICAL**

Democratic Renewal –.

A modern constitution that:

  ➢ Recognises that all individuals are born to society and all have inalienable rights by virtue of being human and not to be granted or taken away but must be guaranteed

➤ Eliminates all vestiges of privilege and discrimination based on wealth, religion, position or any other basis

➤ Recognises that society must provide the benefits of society for all citizens

➤ Affirms citizenship rights on an objective basis and provides the rights of first peoples, citizens, residents and refugees with a guarantee.

➤ Respects Freedom of Conscience not to be violated under any circumstances

➤ Recognises the Right of Self-determination of the people of both Trinidad and Tobago and ends the forced union and establishes a free and equal union between them

Renewal of the political process that:

➤ Ensures that Trinbagonians can directly decide matters that concern them and affect their lives.

➤ Eliminates a political process which allows the monopolisation of political life by big parties or special interests

➤ Funds the electoral process, not political parties or candidates

➤ Upholds the right of all citizens to an informed vote and participate in governance

➤ Enable electors to exercise their right to select

and elect their representatives at all levels and eliminates the imposition of candidates for election by parties

➤ Enables electors to hold their representatives accountable and have the Right of Recall to remove any elected official who fails to represent the interests of those they are to represent

❖ ECONOMIC

A new direction for the economy that:

➤ Allows the people themselves to decide the direction of the economy using natural resources to meet the people's needs

➤ Upholds public right, not monopoly right and the sell-off and privatization of public assets in the interests of corporate profit

➤ Ensures that more to be put into the economy than is taken out with the objective of meeting the ever-increasing needs of the people to childcare and recreation, education, health care, seniors' care and pensions are guaranteed in.

➤ Approaches the financing of social programmes as an investment in the future and not a waste. The priority must not be repaying creditors but not ensuring the necessary social programmes

➤ Prevents the militarisation of the economy with all its attendant dangers

❖ **CULTURE**

Culture must serve the people by:

➤ Promoting and Safeguarding the unity of the people based on humanity and on inviolable rights, regardless of ethnicity, religion or any other consideration

➤ Discouraging and Ending all promotion of hate, divisive and racist and dehumanizing culture

➤ Encouraging uplifting and positive activities, promoting what is best in our past and preserving the contribution of all sections of the population to rich heritage and development of our culture

➤ Sharing our culture with others and that of other peoples with ours

❖ **SOCIAL and the ENVIRONMENT**

Recognising the need to ensure a sustainable social and natural environment for human development by:

Providing security by defending the rights of all by:

➤ People can exercise control over their lives and have their needs guaranteed as the most effective way to ensure their security, including the rights of all to work, education, recreation, health care, etc

➤ The State must do all to guarantee the Right of Safety and Security of All citizens

> ➤ No discrimination because of race, age, gender sexual orientation, region or any other basis must be allowed

Solving the problems of environmental destruction and climate change by:

> ➤ empowering human beings, especially the working people, to control the decisions about what to produce and how to produce it

> ➤ ensuring that environmental issues are approached, and laws are established to protect the natural environment considering what is in the interests of human existence

❖ **RELATIONS WITH OTHERS**

Establishing the relations between Trinbago and all other members of the global family by

> ➤ Operating on a modern foreign policy based on the principles of the equality of all sovereign states, of non-intervention in the internal affairs of other states, recognition of the right of all peoples of the world to live according to the system of their choice and opposition to all military blocs

> ➤ Working for the democratisation of the United Nations, eliminating all special rights and veto powers of selected states and ensuring its composition to include all nations of the globe on a geographically equitable basis

> ➤ Maintaining mutually beneficial relations with

our Caribbean neighbours with whom we have shared a special historical relationship

➢ Engaging in International trade based on mutual benefit and development, and a withdrawal from all trade deals that do not conform to these principles

➢ Ensuring that Trinbago is a factor for peace and the Caribbean remains a zone of peace, and work for an end to all war the displacement of people as a result of unjust wars and withdraw Trinbago from any aggressive military bodies and arrangements.

Perhaps with the people once more setting the agenda for Project INDEPENDENCE with proposals such as these as a foundation, our nation-building project will be moving to success and the creation of our *Trinbago*.

National purpose once again inscribed on our banner.

BIBLIOGRAPHY

Alexander, Robert J, A History of Organized Labor in the English-speaking West Indies, Westport, Connecticut, Praeger, 2004

Artana, Daniel and Others, IDB Research Project, Trinidad & Tobago: Economic Growth in a Dual Economy, Inter-American Development Bank, 2007, https://sta.uwi.edu/salises/pubs/workingpapers/16.pdf

Brereton, Bridget, A History of Modern Trinidad – 1783- 1962, London, Heinemann Educational Books Ltd, 1981

Camejo, Acton. "Racial Discrimination in Employment in the Private Sector in Trinidad and Tobago: A Study of the Business Elite and the Social Structure." Social and Economic Studies 20, No. 3. 1971. 294-318.

Craig, Susan, Smiles and Blood: The Ruling Class Response to the Worker Rebellion in Trinidad and Tobago, London, New Beacon Books, 1988

Kiely, Ray, The Politics of Labour and Development in Trinidad, Kingston, The Press University of the West Indies, 1996

Mitchell, Roy, Notes Pegasus on April 21 1990, Port of Spain, Roy Mitchell, 1990

Rennie, Bukka, History of the Working Class in the 20th Century – Trinidad and Tobago, Toronto, New Beginning Movement, 1974

Clyde Weatherhead

Williams, Eric, Dr., <u>Inward Hunger – The Education of a Prime Minister</u>, Princeton, Markus Wiener Publishers, 2017

INDEX

NOTES